SNAPS

"IF UGLINESS WERE BRICKS,
YOUR MOTHER WOULD BE A HOUSING PROJECT"
...AND MORE THAN 450 OTHER SNAPS, CAPS, AND INSULTS
FOR PLAYING THE DOZENS

SNAPS

JAMES PERCELAY, MONTERIA IVEY, AND STEPHAN DWECK

2 BROS. & A WHITE GUY, INC.

FOREWORD BY QUINCY JONES

WILLIAM MORROW
NEW YORK

Publisher and author are grateful to acknowledge the use of
the following copyrighted material:
ASK YOUR MAMA: 12 MOODS FOR JAZZ by Langston Hughes
Copyright © 1959,1961 by Langston Hughes. Reprinted by
permission of Alfred A. Knopf, Inc.

It is the policy of William Morrow and Company, Inc., and its
imprints and affiliates, recognizing the importance of pre-
serving what has been written, to print the books we publish
on acid-free paper, and we exert our best efforts to that end.

4

Library of Congress Cataloging-in-Publication Data

Percelay, James.
        Snaps: "If ugliness were bricks, your mother would be a
housing project"...and more than 450 other snaps, caps, and
insults for playing the dozens
     James Percelay, Monteria Ivey, Stephan Dweck.
             p.   cm.
        ISBN 0-688-12896-3
          1. Afro-Americans—Language (New words, slang, etc.).
     2. English language—United States—Terms and phrases.
     3. Afro-American wit and humor. 4. Afro-Americans—
     quotations. 5. Quotations, American. 6. Black English.
     7. Americanisms. 8. Invective. I. Ivey, Monteria. II. Dweck,
     Stephan. III. Title.
     PE3727.N4P47 1994
     081'.08996073—dc20   93-34484
                                                         CIP

Printed in the United States of America

First Quill Edition

1 2 3 4 5 6 7 8 9 10

BOOK DESIGN BY ELIZABETH VAN ITALLIE

To Merrill and Sheela, brother David,

twin brother Bruce, and Noreen O'Loughlin

—JAMES L. PERCELAY

To my parents Abe and Mildred, Kendall Minter,

Claude Ismael, Jim Grant, and Larry Dais

—STEPHAN DWECK

To my mother Ollie Ivey, Beverly,

Waverly, Anthony, Teku, Mary, Pat,

and in loving memory of Waverly Ivey, Jr.,

and Susie Novela Williams

—MONTERIA IVEY

To our editor Will Schwalbe,

who proved that white men can snap

SPECIAL THANKS TO:

Quincy Jones, Bridget Potter, Betty Bitterman,

Jon Rubin, Doug E. Doug

THE "DARK SNAPPER" CREATED BY:

Hype Comics

CONTRIBUTING EDITORS:

Sonya McLaughlin, Lynn Dillard

ADDITIONAL SNAPS WRITTEN BY:

Mark "Faceman" Jackson, Capitol J.

FOREWORD

BY QUINCY JONES

"PLAYING THE DOZENS" is a sociological condition transformed into an art form. It's a deep part of our culture, an oral tradition that dates back to the griots in Africa. The griots were entrusted with maintaining the oral history of a community. It was the griots who helped Alex Haley find his "roots" back in Africa. They say that every time a griot died it was like another library burning down to the ground. There were instances of griots who traveled with musicians and troubadours. When they learned of someone's indiscretion they put it into verse and sang it throughout all the villages— they *signified* on him.

Talking about your mama comes from slavery. (I wasn't there, but this is what I hear.) After the trip through the middle passage, scurvy ravaged many of the slaves. The twelve most damaged were put together and sold at a bargain rate. They were called the *dirty dozens*. The only thing even more degrading than slavery was to be a part of this group. Insulting your mama was meant to make you feel as low as one of the dirty dozens.

Like music, the dozens has lyrics, cadence, and rhythm. The words might seem rough, but you can't take them literally. Similar to the blues, the dozens is a conversion of pain into joy. This battle of words is a song of survival. Slaves practiced the "game" to offset the pain of not being able to express their true feelings in front of their masters.

The dozens is still about maintaining your cool. The point is not to appear emotionally vulnerable. Talking fast and talking smooth are all part of not letting them know you're scared. The game is a form of ritualized entertainment. You can hear it today from kids. Influenced by hip-hop, the rhyming phrases of the early dozens have become one-line comedic insults: "Your mama is so dumb, she went to the movies and the sign said UNDER SEVENTEEN NOT ADMITTED, so she came back with eighteen friends."

Don't think this form of expression is negative. It's a skill that requires verbal creativity, memory, humor, and the chops to deliver your lines. Playing the dozens requires a sophisticated mind. It's not like expressing yourself with a gun, which requires no wit, no strength, no power.

The dozens is a style of humor that enables us to deal with the pain in our lives. It's a serious art and tradition. It's part of our folklore.

CONTENTS

13

INTRO-DUCTION

TO SNAPPING, CAPPING, AND PLAYING THE DOZENS

I LEARNED TO PLAY THE DOZENS just by being black—it was cultural. —ICE-T

My domain for snapping was the high school cafeteria. I used to call a crowd first, because it's no fun when there are only one or two people watching. One day I was ranking on this guy named Ernest. I had a video camera on me and after about six "You're so black" jokes I turned the camera to him and said, "We need more light!" That was the last straw for Ernest. He beat me up. I had it all on camera...and of course this was pre-Rodney King. —DOUG E. DOUG

I learned the dozens (we called it "busting") by overhearing my parents and relatives play it. They used to go downstairs so we couldn't over-hear them, but the walls were too thin. Playing with family or friends is okay, but if you play with a stranger you're playing with fire—you never know what button you might be pushing....As much as we played the dozens as kids, no one ever got so mad that they would fight. We played to laugh and let out steam. However, some got their feelings hurt pretty badly—enough so when they went home that night they would figure out how to come back the next day. —MONTEL WILLIAMS

It was always cool until somebody started talking about your mama. Then it took it to a whole other level. I never played "your mama" jokes. I left my mother out of it. —MALCOLM JAMAL WARNER

I grew up in Chicago, where all the kids played the dozens, but I never played. The words were too real. You've got to be careful when playing the dozens because someone can get hurt—like yourself. —ROBERT TOWNSEND

Playing this game was at the center of my childhood. There were so many battles. I remember hanging out with a friend of mine named Gary Brewer in East St. Louis. There was a barber shop on Eighth Avenue and 128th Street. One night Gary and I went into the barber shop and these guys were cutting heads, and drinking, and playing the dozens. The more they drank, the more they talked. That night I experienced one of the highest levels of comedy I can remember. It's so interesting how we changed our style as we grew older.
 —WARRINGTON HUDLIN

For us playing the dozens was like a mental challenge; a challenge to see who could be the wittiest. But after you couldn't think of any more jabs, your last resort was saying "your mama." Even guys who normally wouldn't fight would be ready to go if you talked about their mama. Now there was one guy I remember named Cornell. He was a paraplegic who usually sat slumped in his wheelchair. But if you started to talk about his mother he'd raise up his hands, straighten himself up, and be ready to fight. —EDDIE LEVERT

We were the first generation of white Irish guys in my neighborhood to listen to black music. We started dressing conservatively, wearing vests, eyelet-collar shirts, slim jim ties, charcoal suits. We would wear wing tips, French toes, and Stacy Adams. Anything to be like the black kids because we wanted to be cool! We just knew there was this great street cool. The dozens was part of that, we called it "slippin."...It was always "your mother."

I always felt the black dozens were gentler and more game-like than what we did. We went for the crotch and the jugular. We didn't say "Your mama," we said "Fuck your mother, fuck your mother in the asshole with a wooden broom handle and break it off!" We were serious. —GEORGE CARLIN

I learned how to talk in the street, not from reading Dick and Jane going to the zoo and all that simple shit. The teacher would test our vocabulary each week, but we knew all the vocabulary we needed. They'd give us arithmetic to exercise our minds. Hell, we exercised our minds by playing the dozens....And the teacher expected me to sit up in class and study poetry....If anybody needed to study poetry, she needed to study mine. We played the dozens for recreation, like white folks play Scrabble.

—H. RAP BROWN, *DIE NIGGER DIE!*

Playing the dozens shows that we care about each other as friends—in our own sort of macho way. It can make you a star, make you feel a little esteem if you can be the cat who can outrank everybody. —LAWRENCE HILTON JACOBS

I don't think it's indecent, I just think it's funny as hell, and dirty. Dirty doesn't have to be indecent. It's bawdy, it's terribly bawdy, and done with shocking power. Somebody's going to be outraged about it, and that's great.

I'm a minister, I'm a pastor of a church, so when they hear my music, my insulting language, my own parishioners know it has nothing to do with being a good person.

The more it surfaces and becomes available to mainstream readers, the closer we come to the day when some whites will take it, maybe make an album of it, and then stand up and claim they invented it—start taking bows as they've done with all other black creations. So I'm terribly cynical and bitter in that direction.
—JOHNNY OTIS

I used to play with Nat Adderley on road trips. He would always wake up early to leave his hotel room in the morning. When I would get up there'd be a bottle of Scope with a note attached saying, "This is for Roy Ayers's mother." —ROY AYERS

There was always an audience while playing the dozens. You had to have it. It's amazing about that behavior. The same person you *capped on* because other people were present, you would leave alone soon as the audience left. It was no fun when there was no one there to respond. —DENNIS JOHNSON, SHOWTIME NETWORKS

In Chicago, we called it signifying....We played it in the schoolroom, in the 'hood, we played it on people's porches, on the court, every-where. We played it. It was a part of life, but we did it with modera-tion. If you destroyed someone's feelings, and I've seen it happen, one of you would quit—"Hey man, cool out. You're getting a little too heavy on that." People were more neighbors back then, you didn't want to just hurt anybody back then....The pain. Snapping is pain. And that's why the guys who are really the best at it have the most pain. You have to be at your worst to be the best at this game.
—BERNIE MACK

SNAPS is the first book of its kind to recognize the African-American game of "playing the dozens" as a comedic art form. Although it is older than jazz, this traditional game of insults is virtually unknown outside the African-American community. Born out of a shared expe-rience of pain and prejudice, the verbal repartee of the dozens remains almost a secret language. However, now that writers are starting to feature "mother jokes" in popular movies, commercials, and television shows, the game is headed for Main Street, U.S.A.

While we view the dozens as a comedic art form, we are aware of the pain from which this humor arises. The roughness of the verbal insults is an expression of these feelings. While readers may find some snaps particularly offensive, such as snaps that refer to skin color or sex, we have presented them just as we found them. Ironically, the focus on "your mother" in so many snaps points to a reverence most contestants share for their mothers. In the dozens, this reverence is used as an emotional weapon.

We collected our snaps from hundreds of people, ranging from popular comedians to kids on the street. We arranged their snaps by the target of their insults, for example weight (Fat Snaps), I.Q. (Stupid Snaps), and dress (Clothing Snaps). Within these categories, the snaps are randomly ordered, just as they would be in a battle of the dozens. Some of the snaps in this book have been written by comedians expressly for this project. However, most were from people who created their own snaps, picked them up from friends, had them passed down from family, or witnessed them in a battle. The celebrity snaps are often their favorites and are not necessarily "invented" by the celebrity. In addition to our interviews, we collected snaps from films, television shows, books, and recorded material.

Fat, Stupid, Sex, and Ugly snaps make up the largest chapters in this book. According to comedians and masters of the game, these subjects get the most laughs. Since winning at the dozens requires the support of the crowd, snappers have come up with more insults from within these categories.

The dozens is the blues of comedy. It is a ritual that crosses generational, regional, and class boundaries. The dozens illustrates the force of the spoken word, and is the ultimate expression of fighting with your wits, not your fists. This oral tradition is another example of the originality and verbal innovation that distinguishes African-American culture.

FROM ASK YOUR MAMA: 12 MOODS FOR JAZZ

They rung my bell to ask me.

Could I recommend a maid.

I said yes, your mama.

They asked me at P.T.A.

Is it true that Negros...?

I said, ask your mama.

And they asked me right at Christmas.

If my blackness, would it rub off?

I said, ask your mama.

Funny, isn't it? Jazz and poetry and playing the dozens.

—LANGSTON HUGHES

HISTORY
OF THE
DOZENS

AFRICAN-AMERICAN CULTURE has often been referred to as an oral culture, one rich with storytelling and verbal repartee. Among the most interesting but least examined of these verbal traditions is "the dozens," a ritualized verbal contest in which the object is to hurl insults or "snaps" against an opponent. The goal of the dozens is to see which individual can devise the greatest number and most effective insults to humiliate the opposition. The loser of the battle is the one who either backs down, runs out of snaps, or loses his cool, which occasionally results in a physical fight.

Some scholars trace the dozens to Africa. For example, William Schechter reported that Ashanti natives were often involved in verbal contests.[1] And Ram Desai wrote that the worst a Gikuku tribesman could do to another is to "mention his mother's name in an indecent way."[2]

However, Middleton Harris in *The Black Book* ties the origin of the dozens to slavery. She suggests that slave auctioneers sold slaves

1. William Schecter, *The History of Negro Humor in America* (New York: Fleet, 1970).
2. Herbert L. Foster, *Ribbin', Jivin', and Playin' the Dozens* (New York: Herbert L. Foster Associates, 1990).

individually. But those that were ill or old were sold in lots of twelve. Hence, the term *dozens*.[3]

Dan Burley, in Herbert Foster's *Ribbin', Jivin', and Playin' the Dozens*, also believed that the dozens originated during slavery, specifically with American field slaves who used the game in place of physical assault on untouchable, higher-status house slaves. The field slaves knew they would be whipped or starved if they harmed the house slaves, so the individual field slaves vented their hostility by insulting the house slaves' parents and ancestors. The name *dozens* then may have derived from the notion that the house slave's mother was supposed to be "one of the dozens of women available to the sexual whims of her master."[4]

There are still other theories that attempt to explain the origin of the term *dozens*. According to Charles S. Johnson's research, the name may have originated from the unluckiness of throwing a twelve in craps.[5] Roger Abrahams noted William Griffin's suggestion that the name *dozens* may derive from a definition of *dozen*, meaning to "stun, stupefy, daze."[6] And jazz musician Johnny Otis recalled

3. Middleton Harris, *The Black Book* (New York: Random House, 1974).
4. Schecter, *History of Negro Humor*.

that the term *dozens* was slang for a bawdy area of Kansas City in the 1930s that revolved around Twelfth Street.

VARIATIONS ON THE DOZENS

The object of the dozens remains essentially the same as it was a century ago in America, but the game's style has evolved. Earlier versions of the game were played in the form of rhymed couplets.[7] Here is a typical version of the dozens gathered from a South Philadelphia neighborhood in the late 1950s:

> Don't talk about my mother 'cause
>   you'll make me mad.
> Don't forget how many your mother
>   had.
> She didn't have one, she didn't have
>   two,
> She had eight motherfuckers look
>   just like you.[8]

Today the dozens, also known as "capping," "cracking," "dissing,"

5. Charles S. Johnson, *Growing Up in the Black Belt: Negro Youth in the Rural South* (Washington, D.C.: American Council on Education, 1941; New York: Schocken, 1967).
6. Roger D. Abrahams, *Deep Down in the Jungle* (Chicago: Aldine, 1963; rev. ed. 1970).
7. Roger D. Abrahams, "Playing the Dozens," *Journal of American Folklore* 75 (1962).
8. Ibid.

and "snapping," not only include the early versions but also contemporary versions. One contemporary form that is practiced throughout the country is the stand-up comedy style that involves verbal dueling and one-line comedic insults.

"Signifying" was another variation on the dozens. *Signification* refers to talking negatively about somebody through stunning and clever verbal put-downs.[9] This technique is gentler than the dozens and was more often used by children. H. Rap Brown, a prominent figure in the civil rights movement of the 1960s, described signifying in relation to the dozens. In his autobiography, *Die Nigger Die!*, he writes: "The real aim of the Dozens was to get a dude so mad that he'd cry or get mad enough to fight....Signifying is more humane. Instead of coming down on somebody's mother, you come down on them."[10]

The classic story of signifying is "The Signifying Monkey." In this fable, a monkey provokes a lion into fighting an elephant by signifying:

> Deep down in the jungle where the coconuts grow
> Lived the signifyingest motherfucker that the world ever know.
> He said to the lion one bright sunny day,

9. Ibid.
10. H. Rap Brown, *Die Nigger Die!* (New York: Dial, 1969).

> "It's a big bad burly motherfucker coming your way.
> I'm going on off in the jungle and stay out of sight.
> 'Cause when you meet it's going to be a hell of a fight.
> But if ya'll two fight, I know you can win."

To inflame the lion further, the monkey continues his signifying:

> "He said your mama was a slut like a dog in a pack
> Running around the street with a mattress on her back."

After his words instigate a vicious fight between the lion and elephant, the monkey runs off into the jungle. There he gloats about having set up this colossal battle. Intoxicated with the cunning of his own mischief, the monkey falls out of his tree and into the jaws of the lion he had just coerced into fighting.

> The monkey looked up with tears in his eyes
> And said, "Please Mr. Lion, I apologize."
> The Lion said, "Ain't no use in apologizing
> I'm going to put an end to your signifying."[11]

Versions of this story end in two ways: one in which the monkey is killed; the other in which he uses his verbal wit to escape the lion, only to continue his signifying. The very existence of two endings of this story suggests an ambivalence about this oral tradition.

11. Foster, *Ribbin', Jivin'*.

As the dozens grew more integrated into the culture, the line between signifying and the dozens grew less defined. Signifying, a verbal system of emotional defense masked in poetry, has moved closer to the dozens, which values the strength of a quick verbal offense.

THE SPIRIT OF THE DOZENS

Today, young African-Americans play the dozens for entertainment and comedic value. However, research suggests that during slavery the dozens was a game that helped one control anger and keep cool in white society. In *Ossie: The Autobiography of a Black Woman*, Ossie Guffy uses an anecdote to highlight the importance of the dozens as a strategy for self-control.

Ossie was born in 1931. She begins her story describing how she and four other children were playing on her grandfather's farm. One boy was hit and, instead of hitting back, started insulting the others with the dozens. Overhearing this, her grandfather lectured and paddled them:

> "When I was coming up," Grandpa said, "I heard about that game, only I heard about it the way it used to be, and I heard

how it started and why it started. It was a game slaves used to play, only they wasn't just playing for fun. They was playing to teach themselves and their sons how to stay alive. The whole idea was to learn to take whatever the master said to you without answering back or hitting him, 'cause that was the way a slave had to be, so he could go on living. It maybe was a bad game, but it was necessary. It ain't necessary now."[12]

Once Ossie's mother found out what had happened, she pointed out that although the boys should not have been using bad words, the game would teach them how to hold their tempers in check.

The emergence of the dozens in popular media indicates its vitality. Played in movies like *White Men Can't Jump, Bebe's Kids,* and *Boomerang,* the dozens has also been featured on *The Arsenio Hall Show, Martin,* the *Uptown Comedy Club, Russell Simmons' Def Comedy Jam, A Different World,* and *In Living Color.* Madison Avenue has begun incorporating the dozens into commercials such as ads for Nike sneakers and Hallmark cards. It is likely that most viewers are unaware that these demonstrate elements of a rich oral tradition.

This lack of awareness endangers its connection to the African-American culture. The dozens was born out of a people who under-

12. Ossie Guffy, *Ossie: The Autobiography of a Black Woman* (New York: Norton, 1971).

stood the need to create humor amidst adversity. While the humor of this historic art form deserves to be shared, its cultural and linguistic value must be preserved. Maintaining the full spirit of the dozens demands keeping its clever prose attached to its bitter past.

—RICHARD MAJORS, ASSISTANT PROFESSOR OF PSYCHOLOGY, UNIVERSITY OF WISCONSIN, EAU CLAIRE

SNAPS

FAT
SNAPS

Your mother is so fat, she's on **BOTH SIDES** of the family.
—FROM *BEBE'S KIDS*

Your mother is so fat, after sex she smokes turkeys.

Your mother is so fat, when I got on top of her, my ears popped.

Your mother is so fat, she broke her arm and **GRAVY** poured
out. —FROM *WHITE MEN CAN'T JUMP*

Your mother is so fat, she has her own area code.
—STEVE WILLIAMS, WJPC, CHICAGO

Your father is so fat, he has to take off his pants to go into his pockets.

Your mother is so fat, she jumped for joy and got stuck.

—K.C. JONES, WVKO, COLUMBUS

You're so fat, you don't **CAST A SHADOW.**

Your mother is so fat, she uses a VCR for a beeper.

Your mother is so fat, she ordered a double room for a singles weekend.

Your father is so fat that when he rubs his thighs together, I swear **I SMELL BACON.**

Your mother is so fat, she irons her clothes in the driveway.

—DAN JACKSON, WKWQ, CAYCE, SOUTH CAROLINA

Your mother's so fat, she has to use a satellite dish as a diaphragm.

You're so fat, you have to go outside to put on deodorant.

Your mother is so fat, **SHE GOT A RUN** in her blue jeans.

—PREACHER EARL & THE MINISTRY

YOUR MOTHER IS SO FAT, SHE PUTS' ON HIGH-HEEL SHOES IN THE MORNING, AND BY THE END OF THE DAY THEY'RE FLATS.

Your sister is so fat, they had to baptize her at Sea World.

—FROM *IN LIVING COLOR*

You're so fat, you have to use a **TRAIN TRACK** for a belt.

Your mom is so fat, they use her underwear for bungee-jumping.

Your mother is so fat, when she stepped on the scale it said, "To be continued." —JAMES THOMAS, WEDR, MIAMI

Your brother is so fat, he's on a light diet—as soon as it gets light out he starts eating.

Your mother is so fat, she couldn't get section 8, she got section 800.

Your sister is so fat, she can't wear X jackets 'cause helicopters keep landing on her back.

Your mother is so fat, she's GOT MORE CHINS than Chinatown. —SHOWBIZ & AG

You're so fat, you need Hula Hoops to keep up your socks.

Your mother is so fat, when she goes to a restaurant she doesn't get a menu, she gets an estimate. —J. B. LOUIS, WBLX, MOBILE

Your mother is so fat, her clothes have **STRETCH MARKS.**

Your mother is so fat, she has two stomachs—one for meat and one for vegetables.

Your mother is so fat, she needs a watch on both arms 'cause she covers two time zones.

Your sister is so fat, she had to let out her shower curtain.

Your family is so fat, I threw a rock through the window and hit **EVERYBODY IN THE HOUSE.**

Your mother is so fat, at the gas station they fill your tires with air and your mother with gas.

Your mother is so fat, they have to GREASE THE TUB to get her out of the bath. —ROBERT TOWNSEND

You're so fat, you have to hop the turnstile twice.

Your sister is so fat, she had her ears pierced by harpoon.

You're so fat, when I fuck you doggy style I'M RIDING PIGGYBACK.

Your parents are so fat, they tried to make love until he looked at her rolls and she looked at his rolls, and they both got hungry and went to Wendy's. —TERRY HODGES

Your mother is so fat, she can bump into people while sitting down.

Your sister is so fat, I took her to the 7-Eleven AND SHE DIDN'T COME OUT UNTIL 12:15.

You remind me of a toilet bowl—fat, round, and full of shit.

Your mother is so fat, cars run out of gas just trying to pass her ass.

Your mom is so fat, I have to take two trains and a bus to get on **HER GOOD SIDE.**

Your sister is so fat, when she puts on a raincoat she looks like a school bus.

Your mother is so fat, she stepped on a dollar and got change.
—ALYSON WILLIAMS

Your sister is so fat she can play Double Dutch by herself.

Your mother is so fat, she has to sleep in a barn with the rest of the cows.

Your mother is so fat, she got hit by a car and the car sued for body damages.

Your mother is so fat, when she falls **SHE NEEDS A CRANE** to get up. —ROGER MOSELY

Your mother is so fat, after making love to her I roll over twice and I'm still on her.

Your mother is so fat, her blood type is Ragu. —TCF CREW

Your mother is so fat, when she dances the band skips. —SPECIAL K

Your father is so fat, he doesn't eat with a fork—he eats with a

FORKLIFT.

Your mother is so fat, when she walks with high heels she
strikes oil.

YOUR GIRL
LEGS ARE SO
COULD
POOL

Your mother is so fat, she can't even jump to a conclusion.

—BIZ MARKIE IN *THE SOURCE*

FRIEND'S
FAT, THEY
HOLD UP A
TABLE.

Your mother is so fat, **WHEN SHE TAKES THE SUBWAY** the train gets stuck in the tunnel.

51

Your mother is so fat, she stepped on the scale and it read, "Fuck it ...they don't pay me enough for this."

Your mother is like the Bermuda Triangle—when kids run around her they get lost.

Your mother is so fat, if she fell out a tree she'd go **STRAIGHT TO HELL.** —KEITH RICHARDS, KJMS, MEMPHIS

You're so fat, the back of your neck looks like a pack of franks.

Your mother is so fat, she got her baby pictures taken by satellite.

Your mother is so fat, she went to the salad bar and **PULLED UP A CHAIR.**

You're so fat, when you were a child you ate your chicken pox.

You're so fat, your belt size is "equator."
—ALONZO "HAMBURGER" LONGHORN ON *SHOWTIME AT THE APOLLO*

Your mother is so fat, her name has stretch marks.

Your mother is so fat, before you make love to her you have to roll her in flour and find **THE WET SPOT.**

Your mother is so fat, every time she comes out at night there's an eclipse. —TONY PERKINS, WKYS, WASHINGTON, D.C.

Your mother is so fat, when she took her dress to the cleaners they told her, "Sorry, we don't do curtains."

Your mother is so fat, when she turns around they throw her
A WELCOME-BACK PARTY.

Your sister is so fat, every time she puts an apple in her mouth people try to roast her.

STUPID
SNAPS

You're so dumb, it takes you an hour and a half to watch **60 MINUTES.** —FROM *WHITE MEN CAN'T JUMP*

Your mother is so dumb, they had to burn down the school to get her out of the third grade.

You're so stupid, it takes you an hour to cook Minute rice. —HEAVY D

Your mother is so dumb, she thought fish bait was how sharks jerk off.

Your father is so dumb, when the judge said, "Order in the court," he said, "I'll have five chicken wings and some fried rice."

You're so dumb, you think Taco Bell is a Mexican phone company.

Your girlfriend is so stupid, the first time she used a vibrator she cracked her **TWO FRONT TEETH.**

You're so dumb, if you spoke your mind you'd be speechless.

Your sister is so stupid, she went to the baker for **A YEAST INFECTION.**

Your mother is so stupid, she thought a lawsuit was something you wear to court.

You're so stupid, on the job application where it said "sex" you put "**TWICE A WEEK.**"

Your mother is so dumb, when you were born she looked at the umbilical cord and said, "Look...it comes with cable."

You're so dumb, you failed *ROMPER ROOM.* —CORTEZ

You're so dumb, the closest you'll get to a brainstorm is a light drizzle.

Your mother is so country, she got into an elevator and thought it was a mobile home. —FROM *BEBE'S KIDS*

Your mother is so stupid, she put Visine on **BLACK-EYED PEAS.** —TCF CREW

Your mother is so dumb, she thought Hamburger Helper came with another person.

Your mother is so dumb, she couldn't pass a blood test.

You're so dumb, you think Beirut was a famous home run hitter.

Your mother is dumb and dyslexic. When I told her to get me some Head & Shoulders, she got on my shoulders and gave me head.

You're so dumb, you think a **HOT MEAL** is stolen food.

Your sister is so dumb, she missed her period and didn't find out until she failed English class.

You're so dumb, you think local anesthesia comes from Brooklyn.

Your mother is so dumb, she went **CORDLESS BUNGEE-JUMPING.**

Your sister is so dumb, she wouldn't get on a Greyhound bus because she's allergic to dogs.

Your father is so dumb, he put a ruler by the bed to see how long he slept.

Your mother is so stupid, she asked what type of jeans I had on, I said Guess? and she said, "Hmmmmm." —ERIC DAVIS

You're so dumb, you wanted to get in the headlines, **SO YOU WIPED YOUR ASS** with newspaper.

Your mother is so dumb, she snuck on a bus and paid to get off.

Your brother is so stupid, he tried to kill Cap'n Crunch to become a serial killer.

You're so dumb, you think **FEDERAL EXPRESS** is a branch of the government.

You're so stupid, you asked for a price check at a 99¢ store.
—FROM *IN LIVING COLOR*

Your father is so dumb, he went to an L.A. Clippers game to get a **HAIRCUT.**

You're so stupid, on the job application where it said "sign here," you wrote "Aquarius."

YOUR BR IS SO THREW A BALL AT

Your mother is so stupid, she thought Boyz II Men was a day-care center.

OTHER DUMB, HE. BASE-BATMAN.

Your sister is so stupid, she thought she needed a token to get on **SOUL TRAIN.** —DEDRA TATE, BIV 10 RECORDS

Your sister is so stupid, I told her to go to the store for two heroes and she brought back Batman and Robin.

Your mother is so dumb, she sat in a tree so she could call herself **A BRANCH MANAGER.**

Your mother is so stupid, she thought O.P.P. was a miracle drug.

Your mother is so dumb, she thought Hammer was a construction worker.

Your mother is so stupid, she tried to drown herself in a car pool.

You're so dumb, you leave your fly open in case you have to **COUNT TO ELEVEN.**

Your mother is so dumb, she failed finger painting.

—D.J. RED ALERT, WRKS, NEW YORK

Your brother is so dumb, he had a nightmare while daydreaming.

You're so dumb, you have a memory like an **ETCH-A-SKETCH** — shake your head and you forget everything.
—SONNY ANDRE, WMYA, NORFOLK, VIRGINIA

Your mother is so stupid, she thought masturbation was a karate teacher.

Your mother is so stupid, she invited three friends over for foreplay.

Your brother is so dumb, he went to Dr. J. for a checkup.

Your father is so dumb, he tried to hail a cab in a subway station.

Your father is so stupid, when the streetlight flashed **DON'T WALK** he froze and got hit by a truck.

You're so stupid, you waited eight days for next week.

Your sister is so stupid, she dialed information to get the number for 911.

Your mother is so dumb, I told her **WE NEEDED GAS** so she farted in the car.

Your mother is so dumb, I told her she lost her mind and she went looking for it.

Your mother is so dumb, she thinks Olde English 800 is a college course.

Your mother is so stupid, she thought St. Ives was a church.

Your mother is so stupid, she got hit by **A PARKED CAR.**

Your father is so dumb, he got locked in the supermarket overnight and died of starvation.

Your sister is so stupid, I told her to page me so she went on the roof and yelled my name.

Your father is so stupid, he thought racism was an Olympic event.

Your mother is so stupid, she went to the library to get A BOOK OF MATCHES.

Your mother is so dumb, she put lipstick on her head to make up her mind.

MOTHER PID, SHE A BACK REFUND.

Your brother is so dumb, he got stabbed in a shoot-out.

You're so dumb, your brain cells are on the **ENDANGERED SPECIES** list.

Your father is so stupid, he went to a fruit stand looking for Darryl Strawberry.

Your sister is so dumb, she took a word out of context and felt guilty because she didn't put it back.

Your mother is so stupid, I asked her to go to the store to buy a color TV, and she asked, "What color?" —DEDRA TATE, BIV 10 RECORDS

Your brother is so stupid, he tripped over a cordless phone. —TCF CREW

Your father is so dumb, he asked his boss how to spell UPS.

You're so dumb, **YOU TRIED TO DIAL 911,** but you couldn't find 11 on the phone.

Your girlfriend is so dumb, I told her, "Drinks are on the house," and she went up on the roof looking for them. —MACIO ON *UPTOWN COMEDY CLUB*

Your mother is so dumb, on the application where it said "don't write below the line" she wrote "okay." —WIL

You're so stupid, if brains were money **YOU'D NEED A LOAN** for a subway token.

Your mother is so dumb, I told her it was chilly outside so she ran out with a knife and fork. —RUSSELL SIMMONS

UGLY
SNAPS

Your mother is so ugly, when she walks in the bank they **TURN OFF THE CAMERAS.** —BIZ MARKIE IN *THE SOURCE*

If ugliness were bricks, your mother would be a housing project.

Your sister is so ugly, she went into a haunted house and came out with a job application. —GEORGE WALLACE ON *THE ARSENIO HALL SHOW*

If ugliness was a crime, you'd get the electric chair.

YOU WERE SO UGLY AT BIRTH, your parents named you Shit Happens.

You're so ugly, I don't have to worry about birth control....Your face does just fine. —KIM WAYANS ON *IN LIVING COLOR*

Your girlfriend is so ugly, she could model for death threats.

You're so ugly, when you were born they put tinted windows on your incubator. —GERRY GRIFFITH, ARISTA RECORDS

Your sister is so ugly, she has to sneak up on her mirror.

Your mother is so ugly, when she looks in the mirror her reflection **TURNS TO STONE.**

Your mother is so ugly, when she moved into her new apartment the neighbors chipped in to buy her curtains.

—ALONZO "HAMBURGER" LONGHORN ON *UPTOWN COMEDY CLUB*

Your brother is so ugly, **WHEN HE SITS IN THE SAND** the cat tries to bury him.

Your mother is so ugly, I wouldn't fuck her with *your* dick.

If God don't like ugly, then you know you're going to hell.

Your girlfriend is so ugly, **HER DOCTOR IS A VET.**

You're so ugly, when you were born the doctor took one look at you and **SPANKED YOUR PARENTS.**

You're so ugly, you stuck your face out the car window and got arrested for mooning. —KIM WAYANS ON *IN LIVING COLOR*

You're so ugly, your family sent you to the store for bread, and then moved.

Your father is so ugly, he went to Friendly's and got punched in the face.

You're so ugly, you give sperm **A BAD NAME.**

Your family is so ugly, it's illegal for them all to be seen on the street at the same time.

Your mother is so ugly, when she goes to the beauty parlor they leave the mud on.

IF UGLINESS WERE A SNOWSTORM,

your mother would be a blizzard. —ALYSON WILLIAMS

Your sister is so ugly, her pet name is Scoobie Doo.

Your sister is so ugly, she has to play *easy to get*.

Your girlfriend is so ugly, you gave her a hickey and got **A MOUTHFUL OF FUR.**

Your little sister is so ugly, she has to trick or treat by phone.
—GLYNICE COLEMAN, EMI RECORDS

Your mom is so ugly, she looks like she went on a crash diet and **GOT TOTALED.**

You were such an ugly baby, when your mother went into labor your father went into shock.

You're so ugly, every time your mother looks at you she says to herself, "Damn, I should have just given head."

SO UGLY,
N'T GET
YOU WERE
ICK.

Your sister's acne is so bad, her tears have to ride 4x4s to get to her chin.

You were so ugly as a child, your mother used to breast-feed you **FROM ACROSS THE STREET** with a slingshot.

I know why you look like a horse, because I saw your mother grazing in the field. —JACK THE RAPPER

Your mom is so ugly, **HER NICKNAME IS DAMN.**

—CORWIN MOORE ON *UPTOWN COMEDY CLUB*

Your head is so pointy, on a film negative it looks like you're in the KKK.

You're so ugly, when you put on a peek-a-boo nightie—first I peeked, then I booed. —DAVID ALAN GRIER ON *IN LIVING COLOR*

Your mother has no neck, and they call her Head & Shoulders.

You're so ugly, you can stick your face in dough and make monster cookies. —TRACEY MORGAN ON *UPTOWN COMEDY CLUB*

You're so ugly, you're like a Taco Bell—when brothers see you they run for the border. —ARTIE ON *RUSSELL SIMMONS' DEF COMEDY JAM*

Your mother is so ugly, she could make **AN ONION CRY.**
—GEORGE WALLACE ON *THE ARSENIO HALL SHOW*

Your mother is so ugly, she has to sneak up on her makeup.

Your mother is so ugly, the tide wouldn't bring her in.

Michael Dokes is so ugly, **HE HURTS MY FEELINGS.**
—RIDDICK BOWE ON HBO COMMERCIAL

You are so ugly that the sun refuses to shine every time you come out. —SIDNEY POITIER AS STEVE JACKSON IN *UPTOWN SATURDAY NIGHT*

Your face is so ugly, IT LOOKS LIKE YOUR NECK THREW UP. —MONTEL WILLIAMS

BIG
AND
SMALL
SNAPS

Your lips are so big, Chap Stick had to come out with a spray.

Your mother's nose is so big, you can go **BOWLING WITH HER BOOGERS.**

Your mother's ass is so big, when she walks it looks like two puppies fighting.

Your lips are so big, they could be a ride at Great Adventure.
—BILL BELLAMY ON *MTV JAMS*

Your head is so big, you have to use a belt for a sweatband.

Your nose is so big, **IT ECHOES WHEN YOU SNEEZE.**

Your ears are so big, you can hear what I'm thinking.

Your head is so big, I have to pull back your ears to get it through the door.

Your face is so small, your glasses look like a windshield.

YOUR LIPS ARE SO BIG, they look like my ass sideways.

Your mother's ass is so big, before God said, "Let there be light," he told her, "Move your big ass out of the way."
—GEORGE WALLACE ON *THE ARSENIO HALL SHOW*

Your nose is so big, it needs a screen so babies don't get sucked in.

Your butt is so big, when you lay down **THE CRACK IN YOUR ASS** looks like a valley.

Your ears are so big, you can hear sign language.

Your butt is so small, you keep slipping into the toilet.

Your mother's head is so big, she has her hair **BRAIDED BY ANGELS.**

Your mother's nose is so big, when she lays on her back it looks like the Bat Cave. —FLEX ON *UPTOWN COMEDY CLUB*

Your lips are so big, when you smile your hair gets wet.

Your mother's lips are so big, **SHE CAN WHISPER** in her own ears.

Your mother's feet are so big, they locked her out of Foot Locker.

Your mother's feet are so big, I can play Double Dutch with her shoelaces.

Your mother's head is so big, she bought a hat, threw it away, and **WORE THE BOX.**

Your mother's nose is so big, she doesn't use tissues, she uses sheets.

Your ears are so big, **YOU CAN HEAR BACON FRYING** in Canada.

Your nose is so big, you can smell farts on the way.

Your butt is so big, when you're told to haul ass you have to make two trips. —DARLENE HAYES

Your tits are so small, you have to tattoo "front" on your chest.

HAIR

SNAPS

Your girlfriend has so much hair on her chest, her tits look like coconuts.

Your mother's arms are so hairy, when she walks down the street it looks like she has Buckwheat in a headlock. —ICE-T

Your mother is so bald, every time she takes a shower, she gets brain-washed. —DEREK "SHANTE" FOX ON *RUSSELL SIMMONS' DEF COMEDY JAM*

Your hair is so short, **IT LOOKS LIKE STITCHES.**

Your mother's hair is so nappy, she has to take painkillers to comb her hair. —BIZ MARKIE

Your mother's hair is so short, it looks like she rolls it up with rice.

Your mother is so hairy, at the family reunion everyone calls her Cousin It.

You're so bald, if you put on a black turtleneck you'd look like a Pepsi. —ERIC DAVIS

Your hair is so short, you need extensions just to have naps.
—DAWNN LEWIS

Your mother is so generous, she'd give you THE HAIR OFF HER BACK. —GEORGE WALLACE ON *THE ARSENIO HALL SHOW*

YOUR MOTHER HAS THREE STRANDS OF HAIR— TWO ON HER HEAD AND ONE IN HER POCKET.

94

COLOR
SNAPS

Your sister is so black, when she eats a Tootsie Roll she has to wear white gloves to keep from **CHEWING HER FINGERS OFF.** —K. C. JONES, WVKO, COLUMBUS

Your mother is so white, she cries milk and farts chalk.

Your father is so black, he could get a job as **A SHADOW.**

You're so black, when you go outside the phone rates go down.

Your mother is so black, they marked her absent at night school.
—RANDY DENNIS, WKYS, WASHINGTON, D.C.

Your mother is so ashy, when she gets out of the shower she doesn't use lotion, she uses Armor All.

—FREDDIE REDD AND CHRIS TAYLOR, WIZF-FM, CINCINNATI

Your sister's so white, she could go to her own wedding naked.

You're so black, when you sit in a car it looks like it has tinted windows.

Your ankles are so ashy, I thought you had on white socks.

Your father is so black, when he stands next to a building he looks **LIKE AN ALLEY.**

Your mother is so black, **WHEN SHE PUTS VASELINE ON** she looks like patent leather.

Your mother is so black, wrap her in plastic and she'd be soy sauce.

Your mother is so black, her friends call her **SKILLET.**

—KEITH RICHARDS, KJMS, MEMPHIS

You're so black, you can suck a dick with your mouth closed.

Your mother is so black, when she opens her eyes it looks like a subway is coming.

Your mom is so black, when she gets cut she doesn't bleed—she just smokes. —JOE TORREY

You're so black, when you pass a bag of charcoal in the supermarket it goes, "Daddy, Daddy."

Your feet are so ashy, it looks like you STAMP OUT FOREST FIRES for a living.

YOUR SIS BLACK, LOOKED' THOUGHT I ASL

Your sister's feet are so ashy, it looks like she's been kicking flour.

—TONY SCOTT, KMJM, ST. LOUIS

You're so black, if they put you in the bottle **YOU'D BE A PEPSI.**

You're so black, when you wear a white T-shirt, you look like a cup of coffee.

TER IS SO
WHEN I
AT HER I
WAS
EEP.

Your girlfriend is so black, if she put on orange lipstick she'd look like a cheeseburger.

You're so black, if you sprinkled salt on you'd look like deep space.

Your father is so black, if I put a stick up his ass he'd look like a Fudgesicle.

You're so black, **THE ONLY DIFFERENCE** between you and midnight is 11:59. —VAUGHN HARPER, WBLS, NEW YORK

Your daddy is so black, they nicknamed him Pitch.

SMELLY

SNAPS

You smell so bad, you need to use Right and Left Guard.

Your breath is so bad, when you talk **HAIRS FALL OUT OF YOUR NOSE.**

If your girlfriend was in the circus, she would be the fly attraction because she smells like shit.

Your breath is so bad, when you talk your tongue goes numb.

YOUR BREATH IS SO BAD, when you talk I can see the words come out.

Your mother's breath is so hot, her teeth have asbestos caps.

Your mother stinks so bad, she smells like two-hundred-year-old wolf pussy.

Your breath smells like Cheez Doodles—light on the cheese and heavy on the doo-doo. —TRACEY MORGAN ON *UPTOWN COMEDY CLUB*

Your mother's feet smell so bad, when she **TAKES OFF HER SHOES** her toenails curl up.

Your breath smells so bad, people on the phone hang up.

Your breath smells so bad, you need a Tic Tac with a battery.

Your breath is so hot, **ONLY YOU** can prevent forest fires.

CLOTHING

SNAPS

You wear clothes from two famous designers, Poly and Ester.

My clothes are wash-and-wear, yours are **JUST WEAR, WEAR, WEAR.**

You have so many hemlines in your jeans, they look like a sheet of loose leaf.

Your shoes are so old, when you step on gum you know the flavor.

Your socks are so old, they look like they were tattooed on your feet.

DIRTY
SNAPS

Your mother's ears are so dirty, I can pull out **ENOUGH WAX** to make candles.

Your mother is so dirty, she gives *me* ring around the collar.

Your brother is so dirty, he loses weight by taking a shower.

Your mother is so dirty, she jumped in the ocean and left a ring around the shore. —RUSSELL SIMMONS

You've got more grease under your chin than the Colonel's chicken fryer. —DAVID ALAN GRIER ON *IN LIVING COLOR*

Your house is so dirty, I was cleaning the ring around your tub when your mother said, "Chill—the rats are gonna have a track meet."

—ICE-T

You have so much dirt on your neck, I thought you had on
A BLACK TURTLENECK.

You're so messy, you ought to write a column called "Dear Shabby."

HOUSE
SNAPS

Your apartment is so small, the roaches are hunchbacks.

Your house is so cold, **THE ROACHES CAN SKATE** across the living room. —KEVIN GARDNER, WDAS, PHILADELPHIA

There are so many roaches in your house, you should make them sign a lease.

Your house is so small, when you eat in the kitchen your elbows are in the living room. —CORTEZ

Your house is so poor, they tore it down to put up a slum.

Your house is so dirty, when I knocked down a spider web your mother yelled, "Who tore my curtains?" —ALONZO "HAMBURGER" LONGHORN

Your family is so poor, you have more candles in your house than a Catholic church.

I went to your house, stepped on **A CIGARETTE**, and your mother screamed, "Who turned off the heat?" —ICE-T

Your house is so hot, the roaches carry canteens. —FREDDIE PRINZE

Your apartment is so small, when I put a key in the lock I broke a window.

Your house is so small, I walked through the front door and tripped over the back fence.

Your family is so poor, your house **HAS A KICKSTAND.**
—MARK CLARK, WWWZ, CHARLESTON, SOUTH CAROLINA

Your house is so small, you have to go outside to change your mind.
—QUINCY JONES

OLD
SNAPS

Your mother is so old, she went to an **ANTIQUE STORE** and they tagged her.

Your mother is so old, she was a waitress at the Last Supper.
—DEDRA TATE, BIV **10** RECORDS

115

Your grandmother's so old, I told her to act her age and she died.

Your grandmother is so old, she wrote the foreword to the Bible.

Your mother is so old, your father ate her pussy and got **FOOD POISONING.**

Your father is so old, he was the promoter of David vs. Goliath.

Your mother is so old, when Moses split the Red Sea she was on the other side fishing.

Your mother is so old, she knew **BURGER KING** when he was just a prince.

Your mother is so old, she's got Jesus's beeper number.

Your mother is so old, she knew the Honey Comb bear when he was a Chicago Cub.

Your mother is so old, she knew Chubby Checker when he was Slim Jim.

Your mother is so old, she knew the Temptations when they were the New Kids on the Block. —MARK OVERTON

Your mother is so old, she eats rust. —FREDDIE PRINZE

Your mother is so old, she still has her ticket stub from the **CHRISTIANS VS. THE LIONS.**

Your mother is so old, she remembers the Grand Canyon when it was a hidden valley.

Your mother is so old, **SHE HELPED MOSES** edit down the eighteen commandments.

Your mother is so old, she owes Jesus food stamps.

Your mother is so old, when the police ask her for I.D. she gives them a rock.

You're so old, you remember Central Park when it was just a plant.

Your mother is so old, her **SOCIAL SECURITY** number is in Roman numerals.

YOUR MOTHER IS SO OLD, HER SOCIAL SECURITY NUMBER IS 1.

Your mother is so old, she can read the Bible and reminisce.

—HUGH MOORE

Your mother is so old, she played jacks with Cleopatra.

—RUSS PARR, KJMZ, IRVING, TEXAS

Your mom is so old, when she gave birth *you* came out with dentures.

Your father is so old, **HE DREAMS RERUNS.** —ICE-T

Your mom is so old, she was there for the first day of slavery.

—FROM *BEBE'S KIDS*

Your mother is so old, **SHE CARRIES GROCERIES** in the bags under her eyes.

Your mother is so old, she wears Confederate underwear.
—FREDDIE PRINZE

You're so old, your tits are a 34-long.

Your mother is so old, her tits give powdered milk. —ICE-T

SHORT
AND
TALL
SNAPS

You're so short, you could work as a teller **AT A PIGGY BANK.** —JEFF FOXX, WRKS, NEW YORK

You're so short, you have to cuff your underwear. —TERRY HODGES

Your father is so short, you can see his feet on his driver's license. —BOB SUMNER, RUSH COMMUNICATIONS

Your mother is so short and black, if she had a red light **SHE'D LOOK LIKE A BEEPER.**

Your mother is so short, she can drown in a puddle. —HEAVY D

Your brother is so short, he can play handball against the curb.

—KENDALL MINTER, ESQ.

Your mother is so short, **SHE JUMPED OFF THE TOILET** and sprained her ankle.

You're so short, you can shave and tie your shoe at the same time.

Your mother is so short, she can walk under a bed with high heels on. —BIG DADDY KANE

Your brother is so tall, he has to bend over so planes can pass.

Your mom is so short, she bumped her head **JUMPING THE TURNSTILE.**

Your mother is so short, she could sit on a dime and swing her legs.

—HEAVY D

POOR

SNAPS

Your family is so poor, they go to Kentucky Fried Chicken to lick other people's fingers. —DOUG E. DOUG

You're so poor, for Christmas your mom bought you a videotape of *other* kids playing with toys.

Your father is so poor, he had to put a Big Mac on layaway.

You're so poor, you wear your McDonald's uniform to church.

Your family is so poor, your mother calls TV dinner trays **HER GOOD CHINA.**

Your mother is so poor, I saw her walking down the street with one shoe. When I told her **SHE'D LOST A SHOE** she said, "No, I found one."

Your father is so poor, I saw him kicking a can down the street, and I asked him, "What are you doing?" He said, "Moving."
—FROM *WHITE MEN CAN'T JUMP*

You're so poor, you don't have a TV, just a View Master with an extension cord.

Your family is so poor, you have to go home and take off your clothes so **YOUR FATHER CAN HAVE PANTS** to wear to work.

Your father is so tight, he can back into a wall and suck out a brick.

—MARTIN LAWRENCE ON *MARTIN*

Your father is so poor, he can't afford to pay attention.

Your family is so poor, **THEY MAKE THANKSGIVING TURKEY** in a Shake 'n Bake bag.

Your family is so poor, they window shop at Kmart.

Your family is so poor, every time I ring the doorbell your mother sticks her head out and yells, "Ding."

Your family is so poor, the last time you had a HOT MEAL was when your house was on fire.

Your family is so poor, the first time you ever had chicken was when your sister had the pox.

YOUR
ARE SO P
GOT
FOR TH

Your family is so poor, they used to have a color TV, until the crayons wore out.

Your pop is so poor, he went to the subway booth and said, "I'm on the guest list."

YOUR PARENTS ARE SO POOR, THEY MARRIED FOR THE RICE.

Your family is so poor, your TV only has two channels—on and off.

Your family is so poor, they used to have housewarming parties for the heat.

Your family has been on welfare so long, your grandpa's face is on **FOOD STAMPS.**

Your family is so poor, you all go trick-or-treating on Thanksgiving.

Your family is so poor, when I asked for something to eat your mother gave me a BLT: bread, lettuce, and tomato.

Your car is so old, they stole your Club and left the car.

Your mother is so poor, I saw her on the street **SELLING LOOSE M&M'S.**

Your family is so poor, you watch TV on an Etch-A-Sketch.

Your family is so poor, when I asked your mother if I could use the bathroom she said, "Sure, pick a corner."

Your car is so old, it needs four passengers—one to drive, **THREE TO PUSH.**

Your family is so poor, the roaches have to eat out or go hungry.

—NIPSEY RUSSELL

Your family is so poor, your inheritance was in food stamps.

—BRIAN ST. JAMES, WTLC, INDIANAPOLIS

Your family has been on food stamps so long, they gave you

A GOLD CARD.

TEETH

SNAPS

Your teeth are so yellow, you brushed with Aim and missed.

Your dentures have so much food on them, Sally Struthers wanted to send them to Africa. —KIM WAYANS ON *IN LIVING COLOR*

Your mother has one tooth in her mouth, and **SHE SNAPS HOLES** in doughnuts for a living.

Your teeth are so yellow, "I can't believe it's not butter."

If I was judging your nationality by the color of your teeth, I'd say you were Irish.

Your teeth have so many gaps, your mouth looks like piano keys.

Your teeth are so yellow, you could spit butter. —IRENE CARA

Your teeth are so black, **WHEN YOU SMILE** it looks like there's a hole in your face.

You're so ugly, you have three teeth—one in your mouth, and two in your pocket. —ERIC DAVIS

YOUR TEETH ARE SO YELLOW, cars slow down when they see your smile.

Your teeth have more tartar than **RED LOBSTER.**

Your grandmother has one tooth in the back of her mouth, and they call her Uno.

Your mother has one tooth in the middle of her mouth, and they call her Chopper.

Your mother is so toothless, it takes her an hour to eat Minute rice.

Your sister is so bucktoothed, she can eat **CORN ON THE COB** through a fence. —MONTEL WILLIAMS

Your teeth are so big, you have to clean them with a shoebrush.

Your teeth are so yellow, your smile looks like a big Twinkie.

Your overbite is so bad, you can kiss a man and comb his moustache at the same time. —DAVID ALAN GRIER ON *IN LIVING COLOR*

YOUR TEETH ARE SO DIRTY, you could drink water and spit Yoo-Hoo. —MIKE ROBERTS, WVEE, ATLANTA

SKINNY

SNAPS

You're so skinny, you have to **TIE KNOTS IN YOUR LEGS** to make knees.

You're so skinny, you could sleep in a pencil case.

You're so skinny, if you grew an Afro you'd look like a black Q-Tip.

—TERRY HODGES

You're so skinny, **YOUR NIPPLES TOUCH.**

Your mother is so skinny, she could hang glide on a Dorito.

—DON POWERS, KPRS, KANSAS CITY

Your mother is so skinny, she could run through a closed door.

Your sister is so skinny, she can dodge raindrops.

You're so skinny, **YOU DON'T HAVE A BUTT**—just an anus hanging on your spine.

You're so skinny, you only weigh 120 pounds with a brick in your hand. —BILL BELLAMY ON *MTV JAMS*

Your mother is so skinny, if she put a plate on top of her head she'd look like a nail.

You're so skinny, **YOU HAVE TO WEAR A BELT** with your bike shorts.

You're so skinny, Sally Struthers sends *you* food.

Your mother is so skinny, she could limbo under a closed door.

Your sister is so skinny, she can Hula Hoop with a Cheerio.

—RICO REED, KACE, LOS ANGELES

EYE
SNAPS

You're so blind, you couldn't find a *brother* in a room **FULL OF MARSHMALLOWS.**

Your mother is so cross-eyed, she walks in circles.

Your mother is so cross-eyed, she went shopping and didn't know what aisle she was in. —SINBAD

Your girlfriend **HAS ONE EYE** and they call her Ida.

Your mother is so cross-eyed, when she has sex she thinks she's part of a threesome.

Your mother's glasses are so thick, she can count molecules.

Your glasses are so thick, YOU CAN SEE THINGS that happened yesterday.

Your sister is so cross-eyed, she can see her own ears.

Your mother is so blind, she has her eye in her asshole and still can't see shit. —BIG DADDY KANE

Your mom's glasses are so thick, she can look at a map and see people waving. —C. S. MORGAN, WQUE, NEW ORLEANS

Your mother has a glass eye with a fish in it. —TCF CREW

Your mother is so cross-eyed, when she cries tears run down her back. —DONNIE SIMPSON, WPGC, WASHINGTON, D.C.

SEX

SNAPS

I heard you were getting sex all the time until your wrist got arthritis.

Your sister sucks so much dick, **SHE CAN SELL HER SPIT** to a sperm bank.

Your father is like cement—it takes him two days to get hard.

Your mother is like an elevator—if you push the right button she'll go down on you.

Just because you **SUCK DICK IN A PHONE BOOTH,** it doesn't make you a call girl.

Your mother is like a doorknob because everyone takes a turn.

— RUSSELL SIMMONS

Your sister has been humped so much, her pussy went platinum.

Your mother is like a library, she's open to the public.

Your mom is so nasty, she has to **PUT ICE BETWEEN HER LEGS** to keep the crabs fresh. —WIL

Your mother is like a shotgun—one cock and she's ready to blow.

—DARRYL BELL

I fucked your momma in a barrel of flour, and the baby shit pancakes for a solid hour. —JOHNNY OTIS

Your dick is so small, you have to **PEE ON YOUR NUTS.**

Your mom is like a race car—she can burn four rubbers in one night. —ARTIE ON *RUSSELL SIMMONS' DEF COMEDY JAM*

I would talk about your father, but I don't want to brag.

The only difference between your girlfriend and a subway is that everybody hasn't ridden a subway.

Your mother has a pussy on her hip, so she can make money on the side.

If you didn't have ears, you'd look like my dick.

I did your momma in the middle of the ocean, frog came up and **SECONDED THE MOTION.** —ROY AYERS

Your sister is so easy, her legs stay open longer than White Castle.

The only difference between your mother and a washing machine is after you drop in a load, a washing machine doesn't follow you around. —ROB MAGNOTTI ON *UPTOWN COMEDY CLUB*

You were jerking off in a plastic bag and someone asked, **"WHAT ARE YOU DOING?"** You said, "Packing my lunch." —ALONZO "HAMBURGER" LONGHORN

When I see a Christmas card that says "ho-ho-ho," I know to address it to your sister.

I could have been your father, but my dog beat me under the fence.

Your dick is so small, **YOU HAVE PENIS ENVY.**

Your mother is like a TV set—anyone can turn her on. —TCF CREW

Your mother sucks so much dick, she has "Trojan" printed on her gum line.

Your father has a split personality. He's both a john and a prostitute —he jerks off, then pays himself.

CLOSE YOUR LEGS—your breath stinks.

Your mother is like a gas station, eventually everybody gets a pump.
—CHUCK VINSON

Your dick is so small, you need tweezers to take a piss.

YOUR SISTER SUCKS DICK SO GOOD, I HAD TO PULL THE SHEETS OUT OF MY ASS.

Your dick is so small, if I took it to court they'd throw it out for lack of evidence.

When it comes to sex, your sister is **LIKE A CAMEL**—two humps and I'm out.

Your mother is so nasty, she thought a washer-dryer was a douche bag and a towel.

Your dick is so small, it looks like **KIBBLES N' BITS.**

Your mother has wooden tits and breast-feeds beavers.

They say beauty is only skin deep, **SO MAY I PEEL YOU BACK** to get to the good part?

Your mother has so many crabs she walks sideways.

So you want to play the dozens, well the dozens is the game, but the way I fuck your mother is a goddamn shame. —GEORGE CARLIN

Your mother's tits are so big, she has a two-yard advantage in the hundred-yard dash. —VINCE BAILEY, KIPR, LITTLE ROCK

Your dick is so small, it looks like you have two belly buttons.

Your sister sucks dick so well, they call her Hoover Upright.

I'm jealous of your mom because she has a dick bigger than mine.

—DAVEY D., KMEL, SAN FRANCISCO

Your sister is so loose, **SHE'S LIKE A BUFFET**— everyone can help themselves.

Your mother is so easy, she carries a mattress on her back.

—LYNN TOLLIVER, WZAK, CLEVELAND

Your dick is so small, it couldn't break a Cheerio. —RONDA FOWLER

Your sister is so loose, her gynecologist had to treat her for chapped lips.

YOU'RE SO HORNY, the last time you felt a breast it came out of a KFC bucket.

You're so gay, you joined the army because you heard there was a Fort Dix.

Tell your mother to stop wearing different colored lipsticks, because I'm getting **A RAINBOW AROUND MY DICK.**

MASTERING THE
ART OF
PLAYING THE
DOZENS

PLAYING THE DOZENS is more than a game of fun—it is a battle for respect. It is an exhibition of emotional strength and verbal agility, a confrontation of wits instead of fists. The dozens is a war of words—perhaps the best type of war there is.

Across the country there are many names for playing the dozens, such as *capping, cracking, bagging, dissing, hiking, joning, ranking, ribbing, serving, signifying, slipping, sounding,* and *snapping.* While the names vary, the rules of the game remain the same.

This verbal tradition combines elements of boxing, chess, and poetry. In a contest demanding the poise and power of a boxer, the aim is not just to win but to deliver a knockout. Fought before a crowd, the verbal pugilist wants not only his opponent but all who witness to think twice about confronting him or her again.

Like chess, playing the dozens requires a strategy. To win a battle, you must stay two or three snaps ahead of your opponent. Even as you are being attacked, you should be setting up your counter-snaps. Should I say something about his Fayva shoes? Or perhaps attack his fat sister? I'll save my best shot for his Kmart cologne. This is the type of strategic thinking that makes a master snapper.

Painting humorous pictures of your opponent through words is key to becoming a dozens laureate. "You're so fat, your blood type is Ragu" is an actual snap fired in a legendary battle at New York's Frederick Douglass Projects. The picture created by this verbal H-bomb still haunts the victim to this day.

Snaps have to be delivered properly in order to work effectively. The *setup:* "Your mother is so fat..." is a classic example of how to *cock the hammer* for the ensuing *snap:* "...she broke her arm and gravy poured out." Like the firing of an individual snap, the delivery of a series of snaps requires a rhythm. You might loft your initial snaps slowly, then fire the successive barrage with increasing speed.

Members of the audience serve a number of fundamental roles in playing the dozens. First, they are needed to witness the event. Playing the dozens without an audience is like launching fireworks in daylight. Second, they are responsible for recording the verbal history of the battle, and then for spreading it throughout the community. Third, they fuel the conflict by responding to the snaps, and it is their reaction that determines the ultimate winner.

HOW DO YOU GET THE AUDIENCE ON YOUR SIDE? Drawing the crowd's laughter at your opponent is what wins battles. To elicit laughter, you must recognize what makes the audience laugh. First, your snaps must be clever, original, and appear crafted just for your opponent. Second, a snap that touches a shared reality is a good bet. For example: "Your family is so poor, your father's face is on food stamps." Third, after snapping, you should occasionally eye the crowd. This will keep them laughing at your snaps, in fear of becoming a target if they don't.

WHY IS "YOUR MOTHER" SO OFTEN THE SUBJECT OF SNAPS? Like the proverbial "Mom" tattooed on a sailor's arm, there is

nothing more dear to a man than his mother. Mother snaps go to the soft underbelly of your opponent. In the early days of snapping, mother jokes were the big guns. Their deployment was saved as a last resort—one that often elicited the response "Don't talk about my mother!" Nowadays, "your mother" is a stylized opening of most snaps. In fact, they are also commonly referred to as mother jokes.

WHEN I WATCH AN N.B.A. GAME AND HEAR PLAYERS "TALKING TRASH," IS THAT THE DOZENS? Talking trash and basketball are becoming as synonymous as fighting and hockey. It is important to note that "trash talk" is not a version of the dozens—rather, just a prelude to the game. On the streets, if a ball player insults an opponent's shooting, the war of words may escalate into a battle of the dozens. Unlike the dozens, trash talk has no rules, defined sentence structure, audience interplay, or rhythm. Nevertheless, this form of verbal sparring offers insight into the power of words.

WHERE IS THE DOZENS PLAYED? In a playground, on a subway, at a pizza parlor, in a classroom, on a street corner, in a locker room...anywhere peers hang out. A game of the dozens can be sparked by contact on the court or words exchanged on the street. Increasingly, you can see the dozens played in comedy clubs as comedians defend themselves against audience hecklers. Some comedians get more laughs from snapping on the audience than from their routines.

WHAT IS THE DISTANCE THAT I SHOULD MAINTAIN BETWEEN MYSELF AND MY OPPONENT? You may get as close as you want to your opponent without making physical contact. Spatial relations are an important aspect of the game. You can use distance to heighten the effect of a snap. A snap punctuated by a hip shake, fluttering eyes, or lewd hand motion needs space for the audience to appreciate the effect of your body language. When the snap is composed of words alone, closing in on your opponent may enhance the power of the attack.

DO WOMEN PLAY THE DOZENS? Historically the dozens has been a male experience, but increasingly women are playing. Fortunately for men, most battles remain within the sexes.

WHAT DO YOU WEAR WHEN PLAYING THE DOZENS? It is smart to wear clothes that do not give ammunition to your opponent. Battling while wearing a strange outfit could be a death wish. If you sense that you might be drawn into the dozens on any given day, be prepared not only with your wit but with your wardrobe.

DO YOU NEED A LOUD VOICE TO WIN A BATTLE? No. What is important is that you be aware of what kind of voice you have, and use it to your advantage. If you are soft-spoken, do not try to yell. The audience will misinterpret the straining of your voice as a sign that your opponent is landing his snaps effectively. Instead, speak softly and carry a big snap.

In short, the dozens is a thinking person's game. However, the tradition lives on because the game has soul. Ultimately, mastery of the dozens demands that you go to that place where humor, anger, joy, and pain all reside. It is from that cauldron that the greatest snaps are born and delivered.

THE AMAZING ADVENTURES

Wherever evil lurks, one man stands ready to meet the challenge armed with his wits and not his fists...

OF THE DARK SNAPPER

ACKNOWLEDGMENTS

THANKS TO THE FOLLOWING PEOPLE FOR THEIR CREATIVE CONTRIBUTIONS AND SUPPORT: Debbie Allen / Flo Anthony / Roy Ayers / Darryl Bell / Bill Bellamy / Glenn Berenbeim / Andre Brown / Kevin Brown / Irene Cara / George Carlin / Ellen Cleghorne / Glynice Coleman / Eric Davis / Dr. Dre / Herbert Foster / Gangstar / Gerry Griffith / Bill Gross / Guru / Austin Hearst / Heavy D / Steve Hewitt / Ice-T / Jack the Rapper / Lawrence Hilton Jacobs / Dennis Johnson / Mario Joyner / Big Daddy Kane / Eddie Levert / Dawnn Lewis / Michael Lewittes / Jim McGee / Bernie Mack / Allen Marchioni / Bill Miller / Paul Mooney / Roger Mosley / Wendy Moten / Johnny Otis / Bruce Paisner / Judy Pastore / Brett Ratner / Chris Rock / Michael Rudell, Esq. / Mary Salter / Jim Signorelli / Russell Simmons / Sinbad / Anna Southall / Chuck Sutton / Kim Swann / Rosemary Sykes / Dedra Tate / Robert Townsend / Melvin Van Peebles / Malcolm Jamal Warner / Mary Ann Watson / Alyson Williams / Montel Williams / Terrie Williams Agency / Frank Wolf / Haydn Wright

AND THANKS TO THOSE WHO SNAP EVEN BETTER THAN WE CAN: Sharon Alexander / Vince Anelle / Kenny Bailey / Nicola Bailey / Katisha Baldwin / Louise Barlow / Neema Barnette / Donna Baynes / Lola Yvonne Bell / Louis Bell / Terrence Benbow / Benny B. / Adam Bernstein / John Bess / Big L / Black Filmmaker Foundation / Michael Braver / Brooklyn Mike / Willie Brown / Buckwild / Xavier Cadeau / J. C. Callender / Caribbean Cultural Center / Frantz Casseus / Lesvia Castro / Donald Chapman / Ava Cherry / Lisa Clarke / Yvette Coit / Chris Cohen / Comedy Act Theatre / Joe Cooney / Cortez / Sean Couch / Andre Cousins / Lisa Crosslin / Francesca Crupi / Copper Cunningham / D.K. / Kathie Davidson, Esq. / Diamond D / Albert Dotson, Esq. / Doug E. Doug. / Barry Dufae / Dr. Monica Dweck / Vaughn Dweck / Nabi Faison / Shirley Faison / Fat Joe / John Fernandez / Figman / Lord Finesse / Mark Finkelstein / Flex / Harry Fobbs / Scott Folks / Ronda Fowler / Derek "Shante" Fox / "Socks" Franklin / Sundra Franklin / David Gallen / Dianne Gibbs / Deborah Gittens / Steve Glickman / Carol Green, Esq. / Harlem YMCA / Darlene Hayes / Ernie Hill / Terry Hodges / Jordan Horowitz / Lisa Humphrey / Rupert Ifil / Erroll Jackson / Gary Jenkins / David Johnson / Homer Jolly / Alonzo "Hamburger" Jones / Jamal Joseph / Sydney Joseph / Ada Keibu / William Keller / Barry Kibrick / Brett King / David King / Kool B—The Toothless Lover / Kool Bubba Ice / John Henry Kurtz / Sabrina Lamb / Patricia Lawrence / Wyatt

Lawrence / Rodney Lemay / Jerry Leventhal / McCaskill Communications / Macio / Uncle Jimmy Mack / Johnnie Mae / Rob Magnotti / Chester Mapp / Corwin Moore / Hugh Moore / Tracey Moore / Tracy Morgan / Lonai Mosley / Patrick Moxey / Mugga / Earl Nash / National Black Theatre / Kenny Nealy / John Noonan / Jim O'Brien, Esq. / Mark Overton / Lew Perlman / Al Pizzaeo / Alan Potashnick / Preacher Earl & the Ministry / Ratzo / Lisa Ray / Reisman & Associates / Mitchel Reisman / Andre Richardson / Ray Rivera / Jack Sahl / Tracy Salmon / Tunde Samuel / Zack Schisgal / Neil Schwartz / Judith Service / Gary Sharfin / Showbiz & AG / Sam Silver / Sheri Sinclair / J. B. Smooth / Elliot Sokular / Eric Solstein Productions / Alan Sosne / Special K / Tony Spires / Rob Stapleton / Ali Strange / Bob Sumner / TCF Crew / Barbara Ann Teer / Ernest Thomas / Randy Tibbot / Wayman Tisdale / Paul Ungar, Esq. / Uptown Comedy Club / Michael Vann / Marta Vega / Chuck Vinson / Melanie Wain / Michael Walton / Theobald Walton / Gerald "Mr. G" Washington / Kim Watson / A. G. White / Marchene White / Doreen Whitten / Wil / Kenny Williams / Marco Williams / Ghana Wilson / Richard Winkler / Stanley Winslow / Karen Woodall

SPECIAL THANKS TO SOME OF THE VOICES OF BLACK RADIO WHO KEEP OUR VERBAL TRADITIONS ALIVE:

Vaughn Harper	WBLS	New York, NY
Ken Webb, Jeff Foxx, & D.J. Red Alert	WRKS	New York, NY
Brian Scott	WBLK	Buffalo, NY
Rico Reed	KACE	Los Angeles, CA
Jack Patterson	KJLH	Los Angeles, CA
Donald Lacey	KPOO	San Francisco, CA
Davey D & Kevin Nash	KMEL	San Francisco, CA
Tom Joyner	WGCI	Chicago, IL
Kevin Gardner	WDAS	Philadelphia, PA
Carter Sanborn	WUSL	Philadelphia, PA
Rock Thompson	WAMO	Pittsburgh, PA
John Mason	WJLB	Detroit, MI
Mike Roberts & Carol Blackmon	WVEE	Atlanta, GA
Willis Johnson	KKDA	Dallas, TX
Tony Richards	KMJQ	Houston, TX
Russ Parr	KJMZ	Irving, TX
Skip Murphy	KKDA	Grand Prairie, TX
Donnie Simpson	KPGC	Washington, DC

Hector Hanibal	WHUR	Washington, DC
Randy Dennis & Tony Perkins	WKYS	Washington, DC
James Thomas	WEDR	Miami, FL
Jay Michaels & Randy Patterson	WHJX	Jacksonville, FL
Harold Pompey	WWIN	Baltimore, MD
Roy Simpson, Jean Ross, & Bee J	WXYV	Baltimore, MD
Tony Scott	KMJM	St. Louis, MO
Don Powers	KPRS	Kansas City, MO
Keith Richards	KJMS	Memphis, TN
CeCe McGee & Mark Evans	WHRK	Memphis, TN
T. Wright	WQQK	Nashville, TN
Lynn Tolliver	WZAK	Cleveland, OH
K. C. Jones	WVKO	Columbus, OH
Freddie Redd & Chris Thomas	WIZF	Cincinnati, OH
Tony Green	WQMG	Greensboro, NC
Cy Young	WQOK	Raleigh, NC
Juan Conde	WCDX	Richmond, VA
Sonny Andre & J.C.	WMYA	Norfolk, VA
Morris Baxter & Kim Nelson-Ingram	WMYK	Norfolk, VA
Chase Thomas, Stan Verret, & Cheryl Wilkerson	WOWI	Norfolk, VA
C. J. Morgan	WQUE	New Orleans, LA
Genevieve Steward	KQXL	Baton Rouge, LA
Brian St. James	WTLC	Indianapolis, IN
Dorian Flowers	KMOJ	Minneapolis, MN
J. B. Louis	WBLX	Mobile, AL
Dave Donnell	WENN	Birmingham, AL
Mel Marshall	WVAS	Montgomery, AL
Curtis Wilson	WWDM	Columbia, SC
Dan Jackson	WKWQ	Cayce, SC
Mark Clark & Patrice Smith	WWWZ	Charleston, SC
Vince Bailey & Broadway Joe Booker	KIPR	Little Rock, AR
Paul Todd	WJMI	Jackson, MI
Tony Fields	WKKV	Milwaukee, WI
D. J. Berry	WLUM	Milwaukee, WI

ABOUT THE AUTHORS

JAMES PERCELAY is a writer/producer whose credits include production on *Saturday Night Live's* parody commercials and documentaries on subjects including The Rolling Stones and the Dance Theatre of Harlem. He is a former head of development at Hearst Entertainment and is currently developing a television series for CBS.

MONTERIA IVEY is host and writer of the *Uptown Comedy Club* syndicated television series, as well as host of this Harlem club's live shows. His recent performances include HBO's *Toyota Comedy Festival,* Comedy Central, and *Showtime at the Apollo.*

STEPHAN DWECK is an attorney representing numerous television and film actors, as well as musical artists. He is general counsel for the National Black Theatre and teaches a weekly entertainment law course at Baruch College.

2 BROS. & A WHITE GUY, INC., was formed by the authors to write books and films on America's multicultural uniqueness. The company is currently writing a film script about playing the dozens, and developing television projects for HBO and Showtime.

We would like your comments on this book

as well as your favorite snaps.

2 Bros. & A White Guy, Inc.

P.O. Box 0764

Planetarium Station

New York, N.Y. 10024-0539